NEW

No rain, no water
and other stories

Hannie Truijens

Illustrated by Tizzie Knowles

No rain, no water page 2

You won't trick me page 9

I win page 18

Nelson

No rain, no water

It was hot.
It didn't rain for days and days.
It got hotter and hotter and hotter.

"We have no water to drink,"
said Lion.
"We must dig a water hole.
We must all help and then we can
all drink."

The animals started to dig.
"Come and help," said Lion to Hare.
"I am coming," said Hare, "but
I must go and say goodbye
to my children first."

The animals dug and dug.
"Come and help," said Giraffe to Hare.
"I am coming," said Hare, "but I must go and say goodbye to my wife first."

It got hotter and hotter.
The animals went on digging.
"Come and help," said Fox to Hare.
"I am coming," said Hare, "but I must go and close my door first."

The animals went on digging.
"Come and help," said Tortoise to Hare.
"I am coming," said Hare, "but I must have a little rest first."

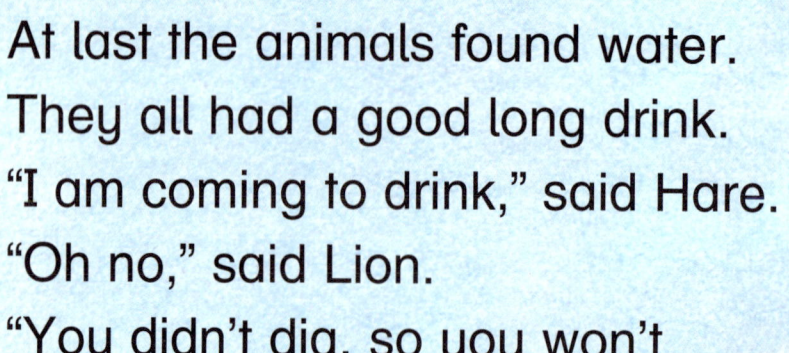

At last the animals found water.
They all had a good long drink.
"I am coming to drink," said Hare.
"Oh no," said Lion.
"You didn't dig, so you won't drink."

You won't trick me

"We must watch the water hole at night," said Lion.
"Hare will come to drink when we are asleep."

The first night Lion kept watch.
Hare came with a piece of meat.
"My dear friend Lion," said Hare.
"Here is a present for you."
Lion ate the meat and Hare went to drink.

The next day the animals went to drink at the water hole.
"Hare tricked you," said Tortoise. "I can see that he came to drink."
"Yes," said Lion, "he tricked me."

That night Giraffe kept watch.
Hare came with some grass.
"My dear friend Giraffe,"
said Hare.
"Here is a present for you."
Giraffe ate the grass and Hare
went to drink.

The next day the animals went to drink at the water hole.
"Hare tricked you," said Tortoise. "I can see that he had a drink."
"Yes," said Giraffe, "he tricked me."

That night Fox kept watch.
Hare came with a big bone.
"My dear friend Fox," he said.
"Here is a present for you."
Fox ate the bone and Hare went to drink.

The next day the animals went
to drink at the water hole.
"Hare tricked you," said Tortoise.
"I can see that he had a drink."
"Yes," said Fox, "he tricked me."

That night Tortoise kept watch.
Hare came with a carrot.
"My dear friend Tortoise," he said.
"Here is a present for you."
"My dear friend Hare,"
said Tortoise.
"I know your tricks."

Tortoise got Hare by the leg.
"You tricked Lion, Giraffe and Fox," he said.
"But you won't trick me. You didn't dig, so you won't drink."

I win

"Hello, Fox," said clever Hare.
"Will you play some games with me?"
The one who wins the most games
will get a prize."
Fox didn't want to play games,
but he did want a prize.
"Yes, I'll play," he said.

"Let's see who can stand on his head the longest," said Hare.
Fox stood on his head, but Hare sat against the tree.
Fox couldn't see this, because he was upside-down.
When Fox was tired, Hare stood on his head.
"I win," said clever Hare.

"Let's see who can spin around the longest," said Hare.
Fox spun round and round, but Hare sat against the tree.
Fox couldn't see this because he was spinning round too fast.
When Fox was tired, Hare started to spin round.
"I win," said clever Hare.

"Let's see who can climb the highest," said Hare.
Fox climbed up a tall, thin tree but Hare climbed up a short, strong one.
Fox's tree started to bend because he was too heavy for it.
"I win," said clever Hare.

"Let's see who can dig the deepest hole," said Hare.
Fox dug his own hole, but Hare found a deep rabbit hole.
"Stop digging now," said Hare.
They used a long stick to see which hole was deepest.
"I win," said clever Hare.

"Let's see who can stay under water the longest," said Hare.
Fox and Hare got into the water.
Fox closed his eyes and held his nose,
but Hare used a reed to get air.
Hare stayed under water much longer than Fox.
"I win," said clever Hare.

Fox was very angry.
"Yes, you win," he shouted.
"But I will get the prize.
AND I will get **YOU**."
Fox ran after Hare, but Hare jumped into the rabbit hole.
"Bad luck, Fox," he shouted.
"I still win."